All for Fall

Whimsical Wool Projects and Warm Quilts

BONNIE SULLIVAN

Martingale®
Create with Confidence

All for Fall: Whimsical Wool Projects and Warm Quilts
© 2018 by Bonnie Sullivan

Martingale®
19021 120th Ave. NE, Ste. 102
Bothell, WA 98011-9511 USA
ShopMartingale.com

Printed in China
23 22 21 20 19 18   8 7 6 5 4 3 2 1

Library of Congress Cataloging-in-Publication Data
is available upon request.

ISBN: 978-1-60468-950-1

MISSION STATEMENT

We empower makers who use fabric and yarn
to make life more enjoyable.

CREDITS

PUBLISHER AND
CHIEF VISIONARY OFFICER
Jennifer Erbe Keltner

CONTENT DIRECTOR
Karen Costello Soltys

DESIGN MANAGER
Adrienne Smitke

MANAGING EDITOR
Tina Cook

PRODUCTION MANAGER
Regina Girard

ACQUISITIONS EDITOR
Karen M. Burns

INTERIOR DESIGNER
Angie Hoogensen

TECHNICAL EDITOR
Debra Finan

PHOTOGRAPHER
Brent Kane

COPY EDITOR
Kathleen Cubley

ILLUSTRATOR
Christine Erikson

SPECIAL THANKS
*Thanks to Julie Thomas of Maltby, Washington,
and Jodi Allen of Woodinville, Washington,
for allowing Martingale to photograph
this book in their homes.*

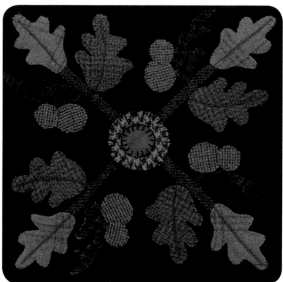

⭐ Contents ⭐

Introduction

I love each season as it comes and goes, from the snowy scenes of winter to the budding leaves of spring to the lazy days of summer that turn into gorgeous fall. And when the year begins winding down, with its golden, nostalgic autumn days, I often think that's the best season of all. It brings to mind one of my favorite quotes:

> "Delicious autumn! My very soul is wedded to it, and if I were a bird I would fly about the earth seeking the successive autumns." ~ George Eliot

There's a feeling of anticipation in the air as the weather turns cool. The changing light, the spicy smells, and the approaching holidays all inspire me to capture fall in whimsical designs. I hope you enjoy this collection featuring warm wool and cozy flannel. If you're new to wool appliqué, take a quick look at page 78 to see how easy it is. Then experience the tactile pleasures as you stitch each colorful project. You'll find friendly pumpkins, squirrels, and cats to keep you company along the way.

Fall is a wonderful season for playing with color. With the bounty of the harvest, it's also a time for giving thanks. The overflowing cornucopia in the Give Thanks table mat on page 18 is a sweet reminder to be grateful. And as crafters we have much to be thankful for—the passion we share, the beauty we can create, and the chance to express our love through handmade gifts for our families and friends.

Autumn truly is a delicious time of year, so choose a fun project, gather some wool and flannel in rich colors, and let's all celebrate fall!

~ Bonnie

Trick or Treat

〜〜〜〜〜〜〜〜〜〜〜〜 designed and made by BONNIE SULLIVAN 〜〜〜〜〜〜〜〜〜〜〜〜

You're sure to delight trick-or-treaters of all ages with this whimsical black cat with a pumpkin. Display him on a wall or on a side table and enjoy him all season long, or you can make a trio of framed pieces, including Scaredy Cat and Mr. Pumpkin Head (page 10).

Finished size: 10" × 13" (excluding frame)

MATERIALS

- 8½" × 9½" rectangle of green wool for background
- 11" × 11" square of black wool for cat, bird, and border
- 3" × 5½" rectangle of brown plaid wool for jacket
- Scraps of wool in gold, orange, white, blue, and purple
- 13" × 16" rectangle of yellow polka-dot flannel for background in frame
- Thread in colors to match wools
- Wool floss in green, pink, gray, white, gold, and red
- ½ yard of 18"-wide paper-backed fusible web
- 3 white buttons, ¼" diameter
- Frame with 10" × 13" opening

PREPARING THE APPLIQUÉS

Referring to "Appliqué with Fusible Web" on page 78, prepare the appliqué shapes using the patterns on pattern sheet 1. Refer to the patterns for which fabrics to use.

STITCHING THE APPLIQUÉS

See page 79 for embroidery stitch instructions. Fuse the pieces in place according to the manufacturer's instructions.

1 Referring to the photo on page 8, arrange the appliqué pieces on the green wool rectangle, fuse, and whipstitch in place using threads that match the appliqué pieces.

2 Using black thread, stitch a combination of straight stitches and outline stitches to make the mouth and teeth lines on the pumpkin. Use a double strand of red wool floss to outline stitch around the mouth.

3 Use a double strand of pink wool floss to satin stitch the cat's nose.

4 Use a double strand of green wool floss to satin stitch the cat's eyes.

5 Use gray wool floss to straight stitch the cat's whiskers.

6 Use a double strand of gray wool floss and a lazy daisy stitch to make the cat's mouth and to outline stitch the handle for the pumpkin.

7 Use a double strand of gold wool floss to outline stitch the bird's legs.

8 Use white wool floss to make French knots on the bird's hat and for the bird's eye.

9 Sew the white buttons onto the cat's jacket.

FINISHING THE FRAMED APPLIQUÉ

1 Trim the appliquéd center to 8" × 9".

2 Place the center on the zigzag side borders, overlapping the straight edge of the borders by ¼". Whipstitch the borders to the center.

3 In the same manner, whipstitch the top and bottom border strips to the center.

4 Space six sets of candy corn pieces evenly across the top and bottom border strips, leaving ¼" clear at each end. The bottom of the gold candy corn pieces should just touch the green center. Fuse in place. Whipstitch the candy corn pieces in place using matching thread.

5 Carefully trim the top and bottom borders a scant ¼" from the edges of the candy corn.

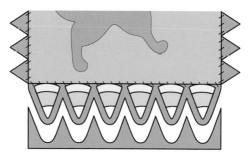

Trim.

6 Center and stitch the penny rug to the green print rectangle. Center the finished piece over the cardboard from the frame and tape the raw edges to the back of the cardboard. Insert the appliquéd piece into the frame.

Scaredy Cat and Mr. Pumpkin Head

designed and made by BONNIE SULLIVAN

The look of surprise on this black cat's face says it all. And who won't be surprised to see a black cat all dressed up in a candy corn hat and purple polka-dotted bow tie? Mr. Pumpkin Head's googly eyes and top hat make him quite the jaunty jack-o'-lantern. This pair of framed pieces works well as a duo or when used with the larger framed Trick or Treat (page 6).

Scaredy Cat

Finished size: 5" × 7" (excluding frame)

MATERIALS

- 3½" × 5½" rectangle of green wool for background
- 6" × 6" square of black wool for cat and border
- Scraps of wool in gold, orange, white, and purple
- 7" × 9" rectangle of yellow polka-dot flannel for background in frame
- Thread in colors to match wools
- Wool floss in green, pink, gray, and white
- ⅛ yard of 18"-wide paper-backed fusible web
- Frame with 5" × 7" opening

PREPARING THE APPLIQUÉS

Referring to "Appliqué with Fusible Web" on page 78, prepare the appliqué shapes using the patterns on pattern sheet 1. Refer to the patterns for which fabrics to use.

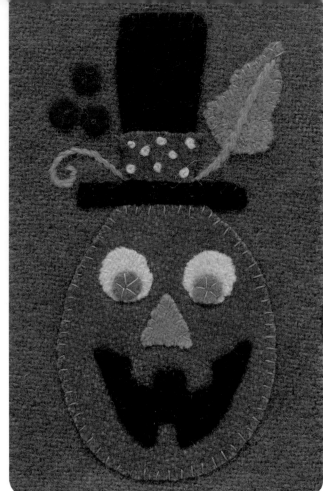

STITCHING THE APPLIQUÉS

See page 79 for embroidery stitch instructions. Fuse the pieces in place according to the manufacturer's instructions.

1 Referring to the photo above, arrange the appliqué pieces on the green wool rectangle, fuse, and whipstitch in place using threads that match the appliqué pieces.

2 Use white wool floss to stitch French knots on the bow tie.

3 Use a double strand of pink wool floss to satin stitch the cat's nose.

4 Use a double strand of green wool floss to satin stitch the cat's eyes.

5 Use a double strand of gray wool floss to lazy daisy stitch the cat's mouth.

6 Use gray wool floss to straight stitch the cat's whiskers.

FINISHING THE FRAMED APPLIQUÉ

1 Trim the appliquéd center to 3" × 5".

2 Place the center on the zigzag side borders, overlapping the straight edge of the borders by ¼". Whipstitch the borders to the center using a coordinating color of thread.

3 Center and whipstitch the wool appliqué to the yellow polka-dot rectangle.

4 Center the finished piece over the cardboard from the frame and tape the raw edges to the back of the cardboard. Insert the appliquéd piece into the frame.

Mr. Pumpkin Head

Finished size: 5" × 7" (excluding frame)

MATERIALS

- 3½" × 5½" rectangle of green wool for background

- 3" × 8" rectangle of black wool for border, mouth, and hat

- 2½" × 3" rectangle of orange wool for pumpkin

- Scraps of wool in gold, white, blue, red, light green, and purple

- 7" × 9" rectangle of yellow polka-dot flannel for background in frame

- Thread in colors to match wools

- Wool floss in light green, white, blue, and red

- ⅛ yard of 18"-wide paper-backed fusible web

- Frame with 5" × 7" opening

PREPARING THE APPLIQUÉS

Referring to "Appliqué with Fusible Web" on page 78, prepare the appliqué shapes using the patterns on pattern sheet 1. Note that the eyes and red berries are not fused. Refer to the patterns for which fabrics to use.

STITCHING THE APPLIQUÉS

See page 79 for embroidery stitch instructions. Fuse the pieces in place according to the manufacturer's instructions.

1 Referring to the photo on page 12, arrange the appliqué pieces on the green wool rectangle, fuse, and whipstitch in place using quilting threads that match the appliqué pieces.

2 Use white wool floss to stitch French knots on the hat band.

3 Use a double strand of light green wool floss to outline stitch the vein of the leaf and the tendril.

4 Use blue wool floss to attach the eyes with straight stitches. Use the red wool floss and French knots to attach the red berries.

A Cut of a Different Color

The beauty of hand-dyed wool is the subtle variation of color. You may want to fussy cut pieces to take advantage of that. For instance, cut the center knot of the cat's bow tie from a slightly darker area.

FINISHING THE FRAMED APPLIQUÉ

1 Trim the appliquéd center to 3" × 5".

2 Place the center on the zigzag side borders, overlapping the straight edge of the borders by ¼". Whipstitch the borders to the penny rug using a coordinating color of thread.

3 Center and whipstitch the penny rug to the yellow polka-dot rectangle.

4 Center the finished piece over the cardboard from the frame and tape the raw edges to the back of the cardboard. Insert the appliquéd piece into the frame.

Dance of the Autumn Leaves

designed and made by BONNIE SULLIVAN

Playful Mr. Squirrel is having fun romping through the leaves on this table mat—just like squirrels do in real life.

Finished size: 15" × 18"

MATERIALS

Fat quarters are 18" × 21".

- 18" × 24" rectangle of black wool for penny-rug background and lamb's tongues

- 6 rectangles, 4" × 8" *each,* of fall-colored wool for leaves and lamb's tongues (green plaid, gold plaid, gold tweed, orange plaid, orange tweed, brown check)

- 6½" × 9" piece of gray wool for squirrel

- 3" × 3" square of rusty red wool for berries

- 2 squares, 3" × 3" *each,* of brown solid and tan check wool for acorns and acorn caps

- Fat quarter of flannel or homespun for backing

- Thread in colors to match wools

- Pearl cotton in black and colors to match leaves

- ½ yard of 18"-wide paper-backed fusible web

- 15" x 20" piece of freezer paper

CUTTING

Using the patterns on pattern sheet 1, make freezer-paper templates of the penny-rug background oval and large lamb's tongues.

From the black wool, cut:
1 background oval
20 large lamb's tongues

From the flannel or homespun for backing, cut:
1 background oval, adding ⅜" all around

PREPARING THE WOOL APPLIQUÉS

Referring to "Appliqué with Fusible Web" on page 78, prepare the appliqué shapes using the patterns on pattern sheet 1. Refer to the patterns for which fabrics to use.

STITCHING THE APPLIQUÉS

See page 79 for embroidery stitch instructions. Fuse the pieces in place according to the manufacturer's instructions.

1 Referring to the photo on page 16, arrange the appliqué pieces on the black wool oval; fuse in place. Whipstitch the pieces using threads that match the appliqué pieces.

2 Using coordinating colors of pearl cotton, outline stitch the center vein and stem for each leaf. Using black pearl cotton, stitch a French knot for the squirrel's eye.

3 Aligning the straight edges, center each small lamb's tongue on a black lamb's tongue, fuse, and whipstitch in place.

Standout Stems

Using pearl cotton rather than thread gives the leaf veins and stems dimension. To help them further stand out, choose shades slightly lighter than the color of your wool.

FINISHING THE PENNY RUG

1 Arrange the lamb's tongues around the perimeter of the penny-rug background with a generous ¼" of each tongue hidden beneath the background. Whipstitch the tongues in place.

2 Place the oval backing fabric wrong sides together with the penny rug and pin. Turn under ⅜" of the backing fabric and whipstitch it to the back of the penny rug. It's not necessary to back the tongues.

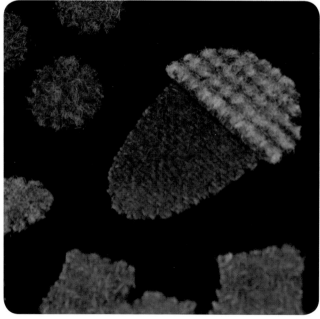

Give Thanks

designed and made by BONNIE SULLIVAN

A cornucopia that's overflowing with fall's bounty will remind you of all you have to be thankful for as you take each stitch on this bountiful centerpiece.

Finished size: 23" × 28"

MATERIALS

- 18" × 42" rectangle of black wool for background and lamb's tongues
- 12" × 20" rectangle of rust wool for pumpkin and large circles
- 12" × 12" square of brown plaid wool for cornucopia
- 8" × 8" square of off-white wool for banner
- 8" × 8" square of olive plaid wool for oak leaves
- 6" × 6" square of yellow-green wool for pears
- 8" × 10" rectangle of green wool for pear leaves, pumpkin stem, and medium circles
- 8" × 8" square of purple wool for grapes and small circles
- 8" × 8" square of brown wool for twigs, branches, and star
- 4" × 4" square of red wool for berries
- 5" × 6" rectangle of yellow wool for squash
- Scraps of light brown solid and tan check wools for acorns and acorn caps
- Scrap of gray wool for back piece of banner
- Thread in colors to match wools
- Pearl cotton in black, green, golden brown, brown, and colors to match fall-colored wools for veins in the leaves (variegated embroidery floss also works well)
- ½ yard of flannel for backing
- 20" × 25" piece of freezer paper
- Paper-backed fusible web

CUTTING

Using the patterns on pattern sheet 2, make a freezer-paper template of the penny-rug background.

From the black wool, cut:
1 background oval
20 lamb's tongues

From the flannel backing fabric, cut:
1 background oval, adding ⅜" all the way around

PREPARING THE APPLIQUÉS

Referring to "Appliqué with Fusible Web" on page 78, prepare the appliqué shapes using the patterns on pattern sheet 2. Refer to the patterns for which fabrics to use. When cutting pieces A–I for the cornucopia from the brown plaid wool, vary the angle of the plaid for interest.

For the twigs and branches, apply fusible web to the wrong side of the brown 8" square and then cut ⅜"-wide strips for stems as needed when arranging pieces for appliqué.

STITCHING THE APPLIQUÉS

See page 79 for embroidery stitch instructions. Fuse the pieces in place according to the manufacturer's instructions.

1 Referring to the photo on page 20, arrange cornucopia pieces A–I in alphabetical order on the black wool oval, overlapping them on the dashed lines.

2 Arrange the pumpkin pieces, pumpkin stem, and yellow squash in place. The bottom of the pumpkin and squash pieces should align with the top of the cornucopia (piece I). Position the oak leaf that tucks behind the squash. Fuse these pieces and the cornucopia

pieces in place and then, using matching thread, whipstitch the rim of the cornucopia in place, covering the edges of the pumpkin, squash, and cornucopia body.

3 Arrange the remaining pieces. Many of the pieces are tucked under others as indicated by the dashed lines on the patterns. Curve and shape the brown strips for twigs and branches as desired. Use the brown strips to shape a five-pointed star, referring to the photo on page 20 for placement.

4 Fuse all of the pieces in place. You'll need to apply pressure with your iron to make the glue melt through the layers. Any pieces that become unstuck can be stapled in place for a temporary hold until you've stitched them securely in place.

5 If you want more definition between the pieces of the cornucopia, use black pearl cotton to outline stitch along the edges of the pieces (optional).

6 Use black pearl cotton to outline stitch the lettering on the banner.

7 Use green pearl cotton to outline stitch a double row of stitches for the grape stem, and a single row of stitches for the veins and stems of the pear leaves, the grapevine, and the pumpkin tendril.

8 Use a matching color of pearl cotton to outline stitch veins on the oak leaves.

9 Use golden brown pearl cotton to outline stitch the twigs that connect the red berries and to add a double row of stitches for the stems that connect the pear to the branch.

FINISHING THE PENNY RUG

1 Arrange an orange, green, and purple circle on each lamb's tongue and fuse in place. Use black pearl cotton to blanket-stitch around each circle.

2 Arrange the lamb's tongues evenly around the edge of the penny rug so that about ¼" of the lamb's tongue is behind the penny rug, and whipstitch them in place.

3 Turn the edges of the flannel backing oval ⅜" toward the wrong side; pin the backing to the wrong side of the penny rug.

4 Whipstitch the backing in place. It's not necessary to back the tongues.

Colors of Fall Table Runner

~~~~~~~~~~~~~ designed and made by BONNIE SULLIVAN ~~~~~~~~~~~~~

The symmetry of this design gives it a bit of a formal flair.
Look closely and you'll see that you've invited not one but two
squirrels to adorn your table! It's a warm, fall welcome for all.

Finished size: 14½" × 43½"

MATERIALS

- 16" × 45" rectangle of black wool for background

- 12" × 13" rectangle of autumn-colored plaid wool for zigzag border

- 6" × 14" rectangle of gray tweed wool for squirrels

- 4" × 8" rectangle of gray plaid wool for vase

- 7" × 20" rectangle of green wool for stems, leaves, and blossoms

- 6" × 10" rectangle of orange wool for pumpkins

- 5" × 5" square of gold wool for pumpkin blossoms

- 4" × 8" rectangle of brown wool for twigs

- 4" × 4½" rectangle *each* of gold plaid and orange plaid wool for leaves

- 3" × 4" rectangle of dark green plaid wool for side-view leaves

- 2½" × 2½" square of light brown tweed wool for puff balls on leaves

- 12" × 41" rectangle of flannel for backing

- Thread in colors to match wools

- Wool floss in green, orange, black, and brown

- 16" × 45" piece of freezer paper

- Paper-backed fusible web

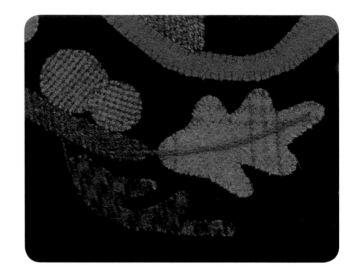

CUTTING

Make a freezer-paper template of the zigzag border pattern on pattern sheet 3.

From the autumn-colored plaid, cut:
8 zigzag borders with 10 points
2 zigzag borders with 11 points

From the green wool, cut:
1 rectangle, 1½" × 20". Apply fusible web to wrong side of rectangle; cut 3 strips, ½" × 20".

PREPARING THE APPLIQUÉS

Referring to "Appliqué with Fusible Web" on page 78, prepare the appliqué shapes using the patterns on pattern sheet 3. Refer to the patterns for which fabrics to use.

STITCHING THE APPLIQUÉS

See page 79 for embroidery stitch instructions. Fuse the pieces in place according to the manufacturer's instructions.

1. Cut an 11" × 40" piece of freezer paper and press it onto the black wool rectangle, leaving a 2½" border of wool around the freezer paper. Using a contrasting color of thread, baste a line as close as possible around the edges of the freezer paper. This will aid in placing the appliqué pieces and zigzag border strips. Remove the freezer paper.

2. Referring to the photo above, arrange the appliqué pieces on the black wool rectangle. Trim and shape the green stems as desired. Arrange the blossoms as shown, beginning with the A piece. Fuse the pieces and whipstitch them in place using threads that match the appliqué pieces. Be sure to keep all of the pieces inside the basted line.

Blossom placement

3. Use a double strand of orange wool floss to outline stitch the lines on the pumpkins.

4. Use a double strand of green wool floss to outline stitch the veins on the green leaves and the tendrils coming off the stems. Use a double strand of matching

Easy Layers

It may not be apparent at first, but the pumpkin blossoms are quite easy to layer and stitch. That's because the two outer petals (A), are actually just one piece. Petal B is simply placed on top of the center of A and then fused in place before stitching. That way you don't have to fuss with arranging three different petals consistently from blossom to blossom.

wool floss to outline stitch the veins and stems of the remaining leaves.

5 Use a double strand of black wool floss and French knots for the eyes of the squirrels.

6 Align the straight edges of the plaid zigzag border pieces with the basted lines on the black wool background rectangle, overlapping the ends of the individual sections. Whipstitch the border pieces in place. Trim away the excess background fabric, leaving ¼" of black wool showing beyond the plaid zigzag edges. Remove the basting.

FINISHING THE TABLE RUNNER

1 Turn the edges of the flannel backing rectangle ⅜" toward the wrong side, and pin the backing to the wrong side of the runner using the basting line as a guide.

2 Whipstitch the backing in place along the line.

Use Your Scraps

If you have a scrap bag of wool pieces, use them here. The squirrels and leaves can all be assorted fall colors.

¼"

Trim.

Oak Leaves Pillow

 designed and made by BONNIE SULLIVAN

Bring the outdoors in! Fall leaves will look even more inviting on your sofa than they do fluttering across your lawn. Perfect for watching television, curling up with a good book, or simply as decor, this crossed spray of oak leaves is sure to be a family favorite. You may have to make more than one!

Finished size: 14" × 14"

MATERIALS

- 2 squares, 15" × 15", of black wool for pillow front and back
- 2 rectangles, 4" × 10" *each*, of gold plaid and orange plaid wool for leaves
- 4" × 6" rectangle of dark green plaid wool for leaves
- 3" × 6" rectangle of light brown tweed wool for puff balls on leaves
- 2" × 4" rectangle of brown wool for stems
- 3" × 3" square of autumn-colored plaid wool for large circle
- 1½" × 1½" square of orange wool for small circle
- Thread in colors to match wools
- Wool floss in black and colors that coordinate with leaves
- Paper-backed fusible web
- 14" square pillow form or stuffing of your choice

CUTTING

From the brown wool:
Apply fusible web to wrong side of wool; cut 4 strips, ⅜" × 4"

PREPARING THE APPLIQUÉS

Referring to "Appliqué with Fusible Web" on page 78, prepare the appliqué shapes using the patterns on pattern sheet 3. Refer to the patterns for which fabrics to use.

STITCHING THE APPLIQUÉS

See page 79 for embroidery stitch instructions. Fuse the pieces in place according to the manufacturer's instructions.

1 Referring to the photo on page 28, arrange the appliqué pieces on one black wool square, fuse, and whipstitch in place using threads that match the appliqué pieces.

2 Use a double strand of wool floss in colors that coordinate with the leaves to outline stitch the veins on the leaves.

3 Use a double strand of black wool floss to blanket stitch around the plaid large circle and the center orange circle.

FINISHING THE PILLOW

1   Layer the pillow front and back pieces, right sides
    together. Sew around the pillow pieces using a
½" seam allowance, leaving an opening in one side
for turning. Trim the corners and turn right side out.

2   Insert the pillow form (or stuffing) and whipstitch
    the opening closed.

Acorn Hollow

designed and made by BONNIE SULLIVAN

Fairy houses and fairy gardens are all the rage these days. Stitch your own fairy-sized acorn house hidden in an oak-leaf woods, complete with sentinel squirrels, a front pathway, and a charming picket fence.

Finished size: 15" × 18"

MATERIALS

- 16" × 19" rectangle of black wool for background
- 13" × 16" rectangle of flannel or homespun for backing
- 7" × 16" rectangle of olive plaid wool for border and grassy hill
- 5" × 8" rectangle of brown wool for trees and chimney
- 3" × 3" square of light brown wool for house
- 2" × 3½" rectangle of brown plaid wool for roof
- 1" × 2" rectangle of gold wool for windows
- 1½" × 1½" square of dark red wool for door
- 2½" × 2½" square of gray/brown tweed for walkway
- 2" × 3" rectangle of off-white wool for fence

- 2" × 2" square of purple wool for flowers
- 1" × 2½" rectangle of green wool for flower bases and flower leaves
- 3½" × 6" piece of gray tweed wool for squirrels
- 3" × 4" rectangle of tan plaid for puff balls
- 3½" × 3½" square of olive plaid wool for leaf
- 3½" × 3½" square of rust plaid wool for leaf
- 5" × 5" square *each* of 2 rust plaid wools for leaves
- 3½" × 6" rectangle of gold plaid wool for leaf
- Thread in colors to match wools
- Pearl cotton in green, black, light gray, and rust
- 1 black button, ¼" diameter, for door knob
- 12" × 15" rectangle of freezer paper
- ½ yard of 18"-wide paper-backed fusible web

CUTTING

Trace the zigzag border pattern for Colors of Fall table runner on pattern sheet 3 onto freezer paper and cut out.

From the olive plaid wool, cut:
2 zigzag borders with 15 points
2 zigzag borders with 12 points

From the off-white wool:
Apply fusible web to wrong side of wool; cut 7 strips, a scant ¼" × 3". Cut 3 of the strips in half to be ¼" × 1½".

PREPARING THE APPLIQUÉS

Referring to "Appliqué with Fusible Web" on page 78, prepare the appliqué shapes using the patterns on pattern sheet 3. Refer to the patterns for which fabrics to use.

STITCHING THE APPLIQUÉS

See page 79 for embroidery stitch instructions. Fuse the pieces in place according to the manufacturer's instructions.

1 Press the 12" × 15" piece of freezer paper to the black wool rectangle, leaving a 2" border of wool around the freezer paper. Using a contrasting color of thread, baste a line around the freezer paper as closely as possible to the edges. This will aid in placing the appliqué pieces and the zigzag border strips. Remove the freezer paper.

2 Referring to the photo above, arrange the appliqué pieces on the black wool rectangle. Fuse and whipstitch in place using threads that match the appliqué pieces. Be sure to keep all of the pieces inside the basted line. The bottom edge of the path and the bottom and side edges of the grass should align with the basting stitches.

3 Use green pearl cotton to outline stitch the flower stems.

4 Use black pearl cotton and a running stitch to add the veins on the leaves. Outline stitch around and through the windows in both directions, making panes. Blanket stitch around the roof, the walkway, and the puff balls. Stitch the black button to the door for a doorknob. Make French knot eyes on the squirrels.

5 Align the straight edges of the plaid zigzag border pieces with the basted lines on the black wool background rectangle, overlapping the excess on the ends. Whipstitch the border pieces in place. Trim away the excess background fabric, leaving ¼" of black wool showing beyond the zigzag edges.

6 Use rust pearl cotton to outline stitch around the black wool rectangle on the basting line.

FINISHING THE TABLE MAT

1 Turn the edges of the flannel or homespun backing rectangle ⅜" toward the wrong side; pin the backing to the wrong side of the mat using the basting line as a guide.

2 Whipstitch the backing in place, covering the line.

Halloween

 designed and made by BONNIE SULLIVAN

Combine your embroidery and appliqué skills in this spooky framed piece. A simple outline stitch is used to spell out the message, which is surrounded by signs and symbols of the season.

Finished size: 11" × 14" (excluding frame)

MATERIALS

- 14" × 17" rectangle of Matka silk in natural for background
- 4" × 4" square of gold wool for moon and candy corn
- 4" × 7" rectangle of orange wool for pumpkins and candy corn
- 4" × 5" rectangle of black wool for crows and mouth on large pumpkin
- 4" × 6" rectangle of green wool for leaves
- 1" × 2½" rectangle of white wool for eyes on large pumpkin and candy corn
- 1" × 1" square of dark gold wool for mouth on moon
- 1" × 1" square of blue wool for eyes on large pumpkin
- 3" × 3" square of dark red wool for berries and noses on pumpkins
- Thread in colors to match wools
- Green pearl cotton to match green wool
- Wool floss in black and brown
- 11" × 14" rectangle of freezer paper
- Permanent marker and FriXion pen
- Light box (optional)
- Paper-backed fusible web
- Frame with 11" × 14" opening

PREPARING THE APPLIQUÉS

Referring to "Appliqué with Fusible Web" on page 78, prepare the appliqué shapes using the patterns on pattern sheet 3. Refer to the patterns for which fabrics to use.

STITCHING THE APPLIQUÉS

See page 79 for embroidery stitch instructions. Fuse the pieces in place according to the manufacturer's instructions.

1 Center the freezer paper on the pattern, shiny side down. Tape at the corners to prevent slipping. Use a permanent marker to trace the lettering, main vine, and tendrils. Note that the pattern is in reverse.

2 To reverse the pattern for embroidery, press the freezer paper to the wrong side of the silk rectangle, shiny side down, leaving a 1½" border of fabric around the freezer paper. Using a light box and FriXion pen, trace the lettering, vine, and tendrils onto the right side of the fabric. The FriXion pen will disappear with the heat from an iron, so don't press the fabric until the embroidery has been completed.

3 Using a contrasting color of thread, baste a line around the freezer paper as closely as possible to the edges. This will aid in placing the appliqués. Remove the freezer paper.

4 Use black wool floss to outline stitch the lettering. Stitch two lines close together for the vertical lines of the letters.

5 Use green pearl cotton to outline stitch the vines and tendrils. Stitch two rows for the main vine and one for the tendrils.

6 Referring to the photo on page 34, arrange the wool appliqué pieces on the fabric, fuse, and whipstitch the pieces in place with matching quilting thread.

7 Use black wool floss to outline stitch the crows' legs and the small pumpkin mouths. Stitch French knot eyes on the small pumpkins.

8 Use green pearl cotton to outline stitch stems for the candy corn and pumpkins and the vein in leaf 1.

9 Use brown wool floss to outline stitch the moon's face and to satin stitch the eyeballs.

10 Frame the finished piece. Center the finished piece over the cardboard from the frame and tape the raw edges to the back of the cardboard. Insert the appliquéd piece into the frame.

Outline and Stem Stitches

The stem stitch and outline stitch achieve pretty much the same look, so you can choose whichever you prefer. For the stem stitch, the working thread is held below the needle, while for the outline stitch, the working thread stays above the needle. That said, when stitching a curve, I think it's important to keep the thread on the outside of the curve, which means that the thread position may change from time to time on a wavy line.

Stars in the Pumpkin Patch

 designed and pieced by BONNIE SULLIVAN

Combine patchwork with simple wool appliqué for a cozy throw comprised of classic Star blocks and vining blossoms. This autumn-themed quilt pairs perfectly with the Pumpkin Blossom Pillow on page 43.

Quilt

Finished quilt: 61½" × 72½"
Finished block: 12" × 12"

MATERIALS

Fabrics used in this quilt are Woolies flannels from Maywood Studio. Yardage is based on 42"-wide fabric. Fat quarters are 18" × 21".

- 3 yards of black windowpane for setting triangles, inner side border, and binding

- 2⅛ yards of olive herringbone for blocks and outer border

- ⅝ yard of gold herringbone for blocks

- ½ yard *each* of gold houndstooth, orange houndstooth, large-scale orange plaid, brown tweed, and brown houndstooth for blocks

- ½ yard of 54"-wide felted olive wool for vines, stems, leaves, and pumpkin blossom bases

- 1 fat quarter of orange wool for pumpkins

- 15" × 15" square of gold wool for pumpkin blossoms

- Thread in colors that match wools

- Olive wool floss to match green wool

- 4 yards of fabric for backing

- Paper-backed fusible web

- 68" × 79" piece of batting

CUTTING

From the black windowpane, cut:
3 strips, 18¼" × 42"; crosscut into 5 squares,
   18¼" × 18¼". Cut into quarters diagonally to yield
   20 quarter-square setting triangles.
1 strip, 9½" × 42"; crosscut into 4 squares,
   9½" × 9½". Cut in half diagonally to yield 8
   half-square setting triangles.
4 strips, 3½" × 42"
7 strips, 2½" × 42"

From the dark olive herringbone, cut:
12 strips, 3½" × 42"; crosscut into:
   48 rectangles, 3½" × 6½"
   46 squares, 3½" × 3½"
7 strips, 2½" × 42"
1 square, 5½" × 5½"; cut into quarters diagonally to make
   4 quarter-square triangles

From the gold herringbone, cut:
2 strips, 3½" × 42"; crosscut into 20 squares, 3½" × 3½"
1 square, 9¾" × 9¾"; cut into quarters diagonally to
   make 4 quarter-square triangles (3 are extra)
2 squares, 6½" × 6½"

From the gold houndstooth, cut:
1 strip, 3½" × 42"; crosscut into 12 squares, 3½" × 3½"
1 square, 9¾" × 9¾"; cut into quarters diagonally to
   make 4 quarter-square triangles (3 are extra)
1 square, 6½" × 6½"

**From *each* of the orange houndstooth, large-scale
orange plaid, brown tweed, and brown houndstooth, cut:**
2 squares, 6½" × 6½"
2 strips, 3½" × 42"; crosscut into 16 squares, 3½" × 3½"

From the olive wool, cut:
½"-wide strips totaling approximately 285" in length
18 leaves and 18 leaves reversed
20 pumpkin blossom bases

From the orange wool, cut:
22 pumpkins

From the gold wool, cut:
20 pumpkin blossoms

MAKING THE BLOCKS

Press the seam allowances open or as indicated by
the arrows.

1 Draw a diagonal line from corner to corner on the
wrong side of each gold houndstooth 3½" square.
Place a marked square on an olive 3½" × 6½" rectangle,
right sides together. Sew on the line and trim away the
excess fabric leaving a ¼" seam allowance; press.
Repeat on the opposite end of the rectangle to make a
star-point unit that measures 3½" × 6½", including seam
allowances. Make four matching star-point units.

Make 4 units,
3½" × 6½".

2 Lay out the star-point units, the gold houndstooth
6½" square, and four olive 3½" squares in three
rows. Join the pieces into rows and join the rows to
complete a block that measures 12½" square, including
seam allowances.

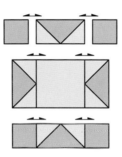 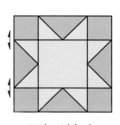

Make 1 block,
12½" × 12½".

3 Repeat steps 1 and 2 to make two blocks *each* with
orange houndstooth, orange plaid, brown tweed,
brown houndstooth, and gold herringbone.

4 Make two star-point units using olive rectangles
and gold herringbone squares and two star-point
units using olive rectangles and gold houndstooth
squares.

Make 2 of each unit,
3½" × 6½".

5 Lay out the gold herringbone star-point units, gold herringbone quarter-square triangle, one olive 3½" square, and two olive quarter-square triangles. Join the pieces to make a half block. Repeat to make a half block using the gold houndstooth.

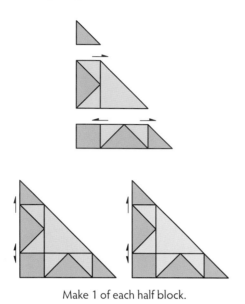

Make 1 of each half block.

ASSEMBLING THE QUILT TOP

1 Referring to the quilt assembly diagram below, lay out four blocks, six black quarter-square setting triangles, and four black half-square setting triangles in a vertical row.

2 Join the pieces into diagonal rows. Join the rows to make row A. Repeat to make a second row A.

3 Lay out three blocks, the two half blocks, and eight black quarter-square setting triangles. Join the pieces into diagonal rows. Then join the rows to make one of row B.

4 Join rows A and B to complete the quilt center.

5 Sew the black 3½"-wide strips together end to end. Measure the length of the quilt center and cut two strips from the pieced strip equal to that measurement. Add the strips to the sides of the quilt.

6 Stay stitch the top and bottom of the quilt, a scant ¼" from the edges.

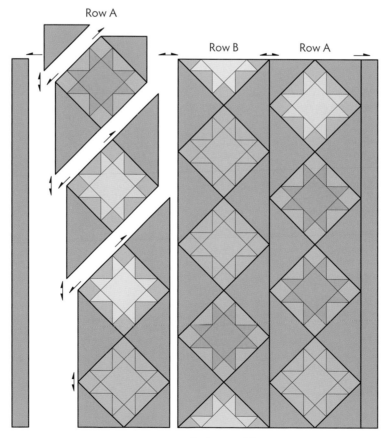

Quilt assembly

PREPARING THE APPLIQUÉS

Referring to "Appliqué with Fusible Web" on page 78, prepare the appliqué shapes using the patterns on pattern sheet 4. Refer to the patterns for which fabrics to use.

STITCHING THE APPLIQUÉS

See page 79 for embroidery stitch instructions. Fuse the pieces in place according to the manufacturer's instructions.

1 Referring to the photo on page 38, pin the vines in place. Position the leaves, pumpkins, blossoms, and blossom bases. Cut stems from the olive wool to the desired lengths and tuck the ends of the stems under the vines and pumpkins before fusing the pieces in place.

2 Fuse the pumpkins, blossoms, blossom bases, and leaves in place. Whipstitch all appliqués in place using thread that matches the appliqués.

3 Use a double strand of olive wool floss to outline stitch the veins on the wool leaves.

FINISHING THE QUILT

For more information on finishing techniques, go to ShopMartingale.com/HowtoQuilt.

1 Sew two olive 2½" × 42" strips together end to end. Cut a side border from the pieced strip equal to the length of the black 3½"-wide inner-border strips. Cut two side borders and add them to the sides of the quilt.

2 Measure the width of the quilt through the center, including the borders just added. Sew the remaining olive 2½" × 42" strips together end to end. Cut two borders equal to that measurement and add them to the top and bottom of the quilt.

3 Layer and baste the backing, batting, and quilt top. Quilt by hand or machine. The quilt shown is machine quilted with feathers in the blocks and with in-the-ditch and outline quilting.

4 Use the black 2½"-wide strips to make double-fold binding, and then attach the binding to the quilt.

Pumpkin Blossom Pillow

 designed and made by BONNIE SULLIVAN

Who needs a pumpkin spice latte when you have your own dash of pumpkin spice with this pillow? Newly emerging pumpkins with the blossoms still attached make for a colorful swirl of color in this punchy pillow.

Finished size: 14" × 14"

MATERIALS

- 2 squares, 15" × 15", of black wool for pillow front and back

- 4" × 6" rectangle of orange wool for pumpkins

- 4" × 8" rectangle of gold wool for pumpkin blossoms

- 8" × 10" rectangle of green wool for stems, leaves, and blossoms

- 3" × 3" square of brown plaid wool for large circle

- 1½" × 1½" square of brown tweed wool for small circle

- Thread in colors to match wools

- Wool floss in green, orange, and black

- Paper-backed fusible web

- 14" × 14" square pillow form or stuffing

MAKING THE PILLOW

1 Referring to "Appliqué with Fusible Web" on page 78, prepare the appliqué shapes using the patterns on pattern sheet 4. Refer to the patterns for which fabrics to use. For the stems, fuse a 2" × 4" rectangle of fusible web to the green wool and then cut four strips, ½" × 4". Fuse the pieces in place according to the manufacturer's instructions.

2 Referring to the photo above right, arrange the appliqué pieces on one black wool square, fuse, and whipstitch in place using threads that match the appliqué pieces.

3 Use a double strand of green wool floss to outline stitch the veins on the leaves, and a

double strand of orange wool floss to outline stitch the lines on the pumpkins. See page 79 for embroidery stitch instructions.

4 Use a double strand of black wool floss to blanket stitch around the brown plaid large circle and the smaller brown center circle.

5 Layer the pillow front and back pieces, right sides together. Sew around the pillow pieces using a ½" seam allowance, leaving an opening in one side for turning. Trim the excess in the corners and turn right side out.

6 Insert the pillow form (or stuffing) and whipstitch the opening closed.

Patchwork Pennies Quilt

designed and pieced by BONNIE SULLIVAN

Stitched in flannel, this cozy quilt will be a favorite all fall and winter.
You'll find the blocks in this quilt are fun and easy to make, and
they yield a powerful visual punch when set together.

Finished quilt: 64½" × 64½"
Block size: 8" × 8"

MATERIALS

Fabrics used in this quilt are Woolies flannels from Maywood Studio. Yardage is based on 42"-wide fabric. Fat quarters are 18"×21".

- 3½ yards of black plaid for blocks and binding

- ½ yard of red herringbone for blocks

- 1 fat quarter *each* of 16 light to medium prints (windowpane, tweed, herringbone, houndstooth, basketweave, and checks) for blocks

- 10" × 10" square of black wool for circles

- 4 yards of flannel for backing

- 71" × 71" piece of batting

- Black thread

- Freezer paper or template plastic

CUTTING

The circle pattern is on page 47.

From the black plaid, cut:
15 strips, 4½" × 42"; crosscut into 128 squares, 4½" × 4½"
15 strips, 2½" × 42"; crosscut 8 strips into 128 squares,
    2½" × 2½". (Remaining strips are for binding.)

From the red herringbone:
7 strips, 2" × 42"; crosscut into 128 squares, 2" × 2"

From *each* fat quarter, cut:
8 squares, 5" × 5" (128 total)*
8 squares, 2½" × 2½" (128 total)*

From the black wool, cut:
32 circles, 1¼" diameter

*See cutting guide below.

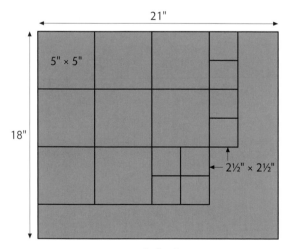

Cutting guide for fat quarters

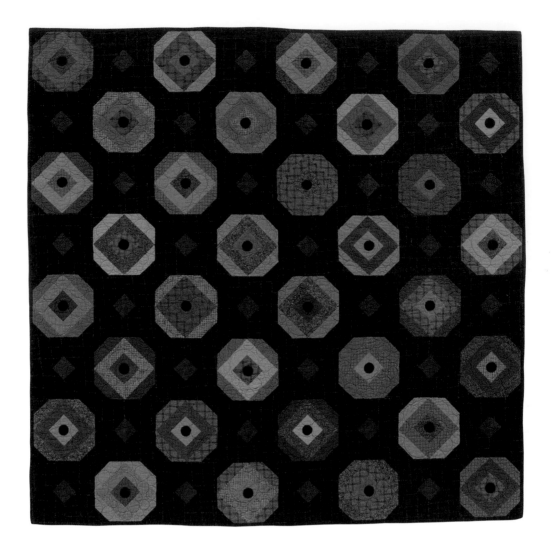

MAKING THE BLOCKS

Press the seam allowances as indicated by the arrows.

1 Pair up all of the 5" squares to make 64 pairs. You will need two identical pairs in each fabric combination.

2 Draw a diagonal line from corner to corner on the wrong side of one square in each pair. Place the pair of squares right sides together. Sew ¼" from both sides of the line. Cut on the line to yield two half-square-triangle units. Trim each unit to 4½" square. Repeat to make a total of 128 half-square-triangle units (32 sets of four matching units).

3 Draw a diagonal line from corner to corner on the wrong side of each black plaid 2½" square.

4 For one block, choose four matching half-square-triangle units and four matching 2½" squares that contrast with the half-square-triangle units. Draw a diagonal line from corner to corner on the wrong side of each 2½" square.

5 Place a marked square on one corner of a half-square-triangle unit, right sides together. Sew on the line; trim away the excess fabric, leaving a ¼" seam allowance, and press. In the same manner, sew a black plaid 2½" square to the opposite corner of the unit. Make four matching units.

Make 32 sets of 4 units,
4½" × 4½".

Make 4 units,
4½" × 4½".

Lay out the four units in two rows with the black triangles in the outer corners. Sew the units into rows, and then join the rows to make a Penny block that measures 8½" square, including seam allowances.

Penny block,
8½" × 8½"

7 Repeat steps 4–6 to make a total of 32 Penny blocks.

8 Pin a black wool circle to the center of each Penny block and whipstitch it in place.

Make 32 Penny blocks,
8½" × 8½".

9 Draw a diagonal line from corner to corner on the wrong side of each red herringbone 2" square. Place a marked square on one corner of a black plaid 4½" square, right sides together. Sew on the line. Cut ¼" beyond the line; press the triangle open. Repeat to make 128 black/red units.

Make 128 units,
4½" × 4½".

10 Lay out four black/red units in two rows with the red corners all in the center. Sew the units into rows, and then join the rows to make a block that measures 8½" square, including seam allowances. Repeat to make a total of 32 black/red blocks.

Make 32 red blocks,
8½" × 8½".

ASSEMBLING THE QUILT TOP

1 Lay out the blocks in eight rows of eight blocks, alternating the Penny blocks and black/red blocks as shown in the quilt assembly diagram below.

2 Join the blocks into rows. Join the rows. The quilt top should measure 64½" square.

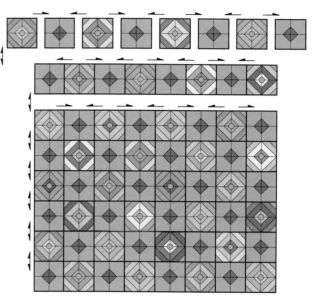

Quilt assembly

FINISHING THE QUILT

1 Cut the backing fabric into two 2-yard lengths. Sew the pieces together side by side.

2 Layer and baste the backing, batting, and quilt top. Quilt by hand or machine. The quilt shown is machine quilted with an allover design of large and small circles.

3 Use the black plaid 2½"-wide strips to make a double-fold binding. Attach the binding to the quilt.

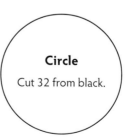

Circle
Cut 32 from black.

Cat and Jack Wool Pouches

~~~~~~~~ designed and made by BONNIE SULLIVAN ~~~~~~~~

Hanging from a doorknob or hook, this whimsical pair is sure to delight with the cat's glowing green eyes and Cheshire smile and Jack's goofy grin.

Cat Pouch

Finished pouch: approximately 7" × 7"

MATERIALS

- 9" × 16" rectangle of dark gray or black wool for pouch
- 9" × 16" rectangle of flannel or homespun for lining
- Scraps of wool in gold, olive, red, dark red, and white
- Thread in colors to match wools
- Pearl cotton in black, white, and gold
- 2 black buttons, ½" diameter
- 54" of black cording for strap
- Freezer paper
- 8" × 8" square of paper-backed fusible web

CUTTING

Use freezer paper to make a template of the cat head pattern on pattern sheet 2.

From the dark gray or black wool, cut:
2 cat heads

From the flannel or homespun, cut:
2 cat heads

PREPARING THE APPLIQUÉS

Referring to "Appliqué with Fusible Web" on page 78, prepare the appliqué shapes using the patterns on pattern sheet 2. Refer to the patterns for which fabrics to use.

STITCHING THE CAT FACE

See page 79 for embroidery stitch instructions. Fuse the pieces in place according to the manufacturer's instructions.

1 Referring to the photo on page 49, arrange the appliqué pieces on one wool cat head and fuse. Whipstitch the pieces using threads that match the appliqué pieces.

2 Use black pearl cotton to blanket stitch the olive pieces to the eyes and to straight stitch teeth lines on the white mouth.

3 Use white pearl cotton and a running stitch to make the whiskers.

4 Use gold thread to sew the buttons to the center of the eyes.

ASSEMBLING THE POUCH

1 Layer the two wool cat pieces right sides together. Stitch around the sides and bottom with a ¼" seam, backstitching at the top edges. Clip the curves and into the V at the bottom of the ears. Turn right side out; press.

2 Stitch the two lining pieces together in the same manner, leaving a 2" to 3" opening in the bottom.

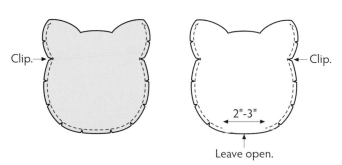

Clip.→

←Clip.

2"-3"

Leave open.

3 Baste or pin the cording to the wool pouch with the ends at the side seams, extending slightly past the top edge.

4 Slip the pouch into the lining and pin the pieces together around the top, matching the side seams. The right sides should be facing each other.

5 Sew around the top of the pouch using a ¼" seam allowance. Backstitch over the cording to secure it in the seam. Trim the ends of the cording that extend past the top edge and clip into the V at the ears.

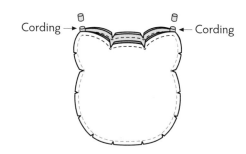

Cording →

← Cording

6 Turn the pouch right side out through the opening in the lining. Sew the opening closed.

7 Tuck the lining into the pouch and press.

Use freezer paper to make a template of the pumpkin pattern on pattern sheet 2.

From the orange wool, cut:
2 pumpkins

From the flannel or homespun, cut:
2 pumpkins

PREPARING THE APPLIQUÉS

Referring to "Appliqué with Fusible Web" on page 78, prepare the appliqué shapes using the patterns on pattern sheet 2. Refer to the patterns for which fabrics to use.

STITCHING THE PUMPKIN FACE

See page 79 for embroidery stitch instructions. Fuse the pieces in place according to the manufacturer's instructions.

1 Referring to the photo at left, arrange the appliqué pieces on one wool pumpkin piece, fuse, and whipstitch in place.

2 Use black pearl cotton to blanket stitch the gold eye circles, the green nose, and the outer edge of the red mouth.

3 Use white pearl cotton to outline stitch lines for the teeth.

4 Use gold thread to attach the buttons to the center of the eyes.

ASSEMBLING THE POUCH

Refer to "Assembling the Pouch" on page 50 to finish this pouch in the same manner, using the orange pumpkin pieces and pumpkin lining pieces.

Jack-O'-Lantern Pouch

Finished pouch: approximately 6" × 7"

MATERIALS

- 9" × 15" rectangle of orange wool for pouch
- 9" × 15" rectangle of flannel or homespun for lining
- Scraps of wool in gold, green, black, red, and brown tweed for appliqués
- Thread in colors to match wools
- Pearl cotton in black, white, and gold
- 2 black buttons, ½" diameter
- 54" of black cording for strap
- Freezer paper
- 8" × 8" square of paper-backed fusible web

Pumpkin Patch Table Mates

 designed and pieced by BONNIE SULLIVAN

Dress up your table all season long with a set of place mats and complementary table runner. The runner's striking pieced border adds a great finishing touch.

Pumpkin Patch Table Runner

Finished table runner: 18½" × 48½"
Block size: 11" × 12"

MATERIALS

Fabrics used in this quilt are Woolies flannels from Maywood Studio. Yardage is based on 42"-wide fabric. Fat eighths are 9" × 21".

- ⅝ yard of espresso herringbone for Pumpkin blocks, sashing, and pieced border

- ⅓ yard of orange houndstooth for pumpkins

- ¼ yard of light green reverse check for pieced border

- ¼ yard of dark green tweed for pieced border

- 1 yard of green herringbone for pieced border, inner border, pumpkin stems, and binding

- 1 fat eighth *each* of 3 prints (tan herringbone, gold herringbone, brown tweed) for blocks

- 1⅝ yards of flannel for backing

- 25" × 55" piece of batting

CUTTING

From the espresso herringbone, cut:
1 strip, 2½" × 42"; crosscut into 12 squares, 2½" × 2½"
5 strips, 2" × 42"; crosscut into:
    2 strips, 2" × 11½"
    80 squares, 2" × 2"
2 strips, 1½" × 42"; crosscut into 2 strips, 1½" × 11½", and
    6 rectangles, 1½" × 6"
2 strips, 1" × 42"; crosscut into 6 strips, 1" × 12½"

From the orange houndstooth:
2 strips, 3½" × 42"; crosscut into 6 rectangles, 3½" × 9½"
1 strip, 2" × 42"; crosscut into 6 rectangles, 2" × 6½"

From the green herringbone, cut:
2 strips, 9" × 42"
3 strips, 1" × 42"; crosscut into:
    2 strips, 1" × 41½"
    2 strips, 1" × 12½"
4 strips, 2½" × 42"
3 squares, 1½" × 1½"

From the tan herringbone fat eighth, cut:
1 square, 4⅜" × 4⅜"; cut into quarters diagonally to yield
    4 triangles
2 squares, 3" × 3"
4 squares, 2" × 2"
4 rectangles, 2" × 3½"

From the gold herringbone fat eighth, cut:
2 squares, 4" × 4"; cut in half diagonally to yield 4 triangles
1 square, 3½" × 3½"
4 squares, 2½" × 2½"

From the brown tweed fat eighth, cut:
1 square, 4⅜" × 4⅜"; cut into quarters diagonally to yield
    4 triangles
2 squares, 3" × 3"
1 square, 2½" × 2½"
8 squares, 2" × 2"

MAKING THE CENTER BLOCKS

Press the seam allowances as indicated by the arrows.

1 Draw a diagonal line from corner to corner on the wrong side of each tan 3" square. Place a marked square on a brown tweed 3" square, right sides together. Sew ¼" from both sides of the line. Cut on the line to yield two half-square-triangle units. Make four identical half-square-triangle units. Trim each unit to 2½" square.

Make 4 units,
2½" × 2½".

2 Lay out the half-square-triangle units, the gold 2½" squares, and the brown tweed 2½" square. Sew the pieces into rows, and then join the rows to complete a Shoofly block that measures 6½" square, including seam allowances.

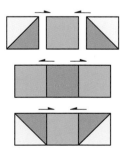 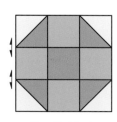

Shoofly block,
6½" × 6½"

3 Lay out a brown tweed triangle, a tan triangle, and a gold triangle. Join the pieces to make a block unit. Make four identical block units. Trim each unit to 3½" square.

Make 4 units,
3½" × 3½".

4 Lay out the block units in two rows. Sew the units into rows, and then join the rows to complete a Pinwheel block that measures 6½" square, including seam allowances.

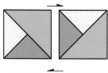
 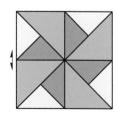

Pinwheel block,
6½" × 6½"

5 Draw a diagonal line from corner to corner on the wrong side of each brown tweed 2" square. Place a marked square on a tan 2" × 3½" rectangle, right sides together as shown. Sew on the drawn line. Cut ¼" beyond the line and press the triangle open. Repeat on the opposite end of the rectangle to complete a flying-geese unit that measures 2" × 3½", including seam allowances. Make four identical flying-geese units.

Make 4 units,
2" × 3½".

6 Lay out the flying-geese units, the tan 2" squares, and the gold 3½" square in three rows. Sew the pieces into rows, and then join the rows to complete a Variable Star block that measures 6½" square, including seam allowances.

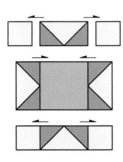 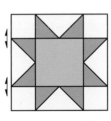

Variable Star block,
6½" × 6½"

MAKING THE PUMPKIN BLOCKS

1 Draw a diagonal line from corner to corner on the wrong side of each espresso 2½" square. Place two marked squares on an orange 3½" × 9½" rectangle, right sides together. Sew on the lines. Cut ¼" beyond the lines; press the triangles open. Repeat to make six side units.

Make 6 side units,
3½" × 9½".

2 Lay out the Shoofly block, two orange 2" × 6½" rectangles, and two side units. Join the pieces to make a pumpkin unit that measures 12½" × 9½", including seam allowances.

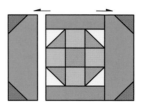

Make 1 unit,
12½" × 9½".

3 Lay out the pumpkin unit, two espresso 1½" × 6½" rectangles, one green basketweave 1½" square, and two espresso 1" × 12½" rectangles. Join the pieces to complete a Pumpkin block that measures 12½" × 11½", including seam allowances.

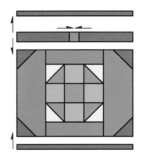 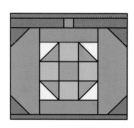

Make 1 block,
12½" × 11½".

4 Repeat steps 2 and 3 to make two more Pumpkin blocks using the Pinwheel and Variable Star blocks for the centers.

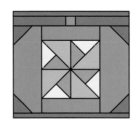 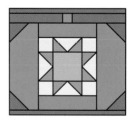

Make 1 of each,
12½" × 11½".

MAKING THE PIECED BORDERS

1 Layer the ¼ yard of light green check and a 9"-wide strip of green herringbone right sides together. Use the 45° line on a rotary ruler to cut five 3"-wide diagonal strips through both layers as shown. Sew both sides of the layered bias strips, ¼" from the edges. Handle carefully to avoid stretching the bias edges. Cut four 3½" half-square-triangle units from each pieced strip (20 total), measuring from the seam to the corner.

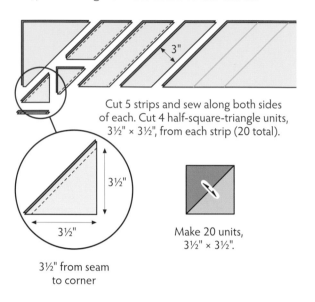

Cut 5 strips and sew along both sides of each. Cut 4 half-square-triangle units, 3½" × 3½", from each strip (20 total).

3½" from seam to corner

Make 20 units, 3½" × 3½".

2 Repeat step 1 using the dark green ¼-yard piece and the remaining green basketweave 9"-wide strip.

Make 20 units, 3½" × 3½".

Pressing Bias Strips

Press the sewn bias strips to set the stitches before cutting the half-square-triangle units. To avoid stretching the strips, press and lift instead of sliding the iron.

3 Draw a diagonal line from corner to corner on the wrong side of each espresso 2" square. Place two marked squares on a half-square-triangle unit, right sides together as shown. Sew on the lines; trim away the excess fabric, leaving a ¼" seam allowance, and press. Repeat to make a total of 20 dark green and 20 light green border units.

Make 20 units, 3½" × 3½". Make 20 units, 3½" × 3½".

4 Lay out three light green and three dark green border units. Join the units to make a side border that measures 3½" × 18½", including seam allowances. Make two side borders.

Side border.
Make 2 borders, 3½" × 18½".

5 In the same manner, join seven light green and seven dark green border units to make the top border measuring 3½" × 42½". Repeat to make the bottom border.

Top and bottom borders.
Make 2 borders, 3½" × 42½".

ASSEMBLING THE TABLE-RUNNER TOP

1 Referring to the assembly diagram below, lay out the Pumpkin blocks, espresso 2" × 11½" strips, and espresso 1½" × 11½" strips (the latter strips go on the outer ends). Join to make the table-runner center. The center should measure 11½" × 41½", including seam allowances.

2 Add the green 1" × 41½" strips to the top and bottom of the table-runner center, and then add the green 1" × 12½" strips to the sides.

3 Add the pieced top and bottom borders to the table runner, and then add the pieced side borders. The runner should measure 18½" × 48½".

FINISHING THE TABLE RUNNER

1 Cut a 25" × 55" rectangle from the backing fabric.

2 Layer and baste the backing, batting, and table-runner top. Quilt by hand or machine. The runner shown is machine quilted with vines and leaves in the border. The blocks are quilted in the ditch.

3 Use the green basketweave 2½"-wide strips to make a double-fold binding, and then attach the binding to the quilt.

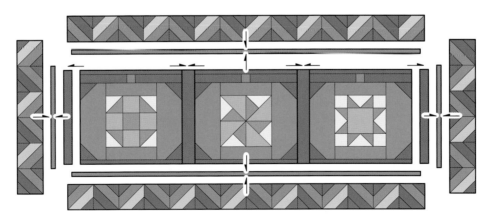

Table-runner assembly

Pumpkin Patch Place Mats

Finished place mat: 17" × 14"

MATERIALS

Fabrics used in this quilt are Woolies flannels from Maywood Studio. Yardage is based on 42"-wide fabric. Fat quarters are 18" × 21". Yardage given is enough for four place mats.

- ⅝ yard of espresso herringbone for Pumpkin blocks and borders

- ⅜ yard of orange herringbone for pumpkins

- 1 fat quarter *each* of 3 prints (cream herringbone, gold herringbone, brown tweed) for blocks

- ½ yard of green herringbone for stems and borders

- 1 yard of flannel for backing

- 4 pieces of batting, 21" × 18"

CUTTING

Cutting is for 4 place mats.

From the espresso herringbone, cut:
1 strip, 2½" × 42"; crosscut into 16 squares, 2½" × 2½"
3 strips, 2¼" × 42"; crosscut into 8 rectangles, 2¼" × 13"
3 strips, 1¾" × 42"; crosscut into 8 rectangles, 1¾" × 12½"
2 strips, 1½" × 42"; crosscut into 8 rectangles, 1½" × 6"

From the orange herringbone, cut:
2 strips, 3½" × 42"; crosscut into 8 rectangles, 3½" × 9½"
2 strips, 2" × 42"; crosscut into 8 rectangles, 2" × 6½"

From the cream herringbone fat quarter, cut:
1 square, 4⅜" × 4⅜"; cut into quarters diagonally to yield 4 triangles
2 squares, 3" × 3"
4 squares, 2½" × 2½"
4 squares, 2" × 2"
4 rectangles, 2" × 3½"

From the gold herringbone fat quarter, cut:
2 squares, 4" × 4"; cut in half diagonally to yield 4 triangles
3 squares, 3½" × 3½"
4 squares, 2½" × 2½"

From the brown tweed fat quarter, cut:
1 square, 4⅜" × 4⅜"; cut into quarters diagonally to yield 4 triangles
2 squares, 3½" × 3½"
2 squares, 3" × 3"
2 squares, 2½" × 2½"
8 squares, 2" × 2"

From the green herringbone fat quarter, cut:
8 strips, 1¼" × 42"; crosscut into:
    8 strips, 1¼" × 16"
    8 strips, 1¼" × 14½"
4 squares, 1½" × 1½"

From the backing flannel, cut:
2 strips, 14½" × 42"; crosscut into 8 rectangles, 9¼" × 14½"

MAKING THE CENTER BLOCKS

Press the seam allowances as indicated by the arrows.

1. Draw a diagonal line from corner to corner on the wrong side of two gold 3½" squares. Place a marked square on a brown tweed 3½" square, right sides together. Sew ¼" from both sides of the line. Cut on the line to yield two half-square-triangle units. Make four identical half-square-triangle units.

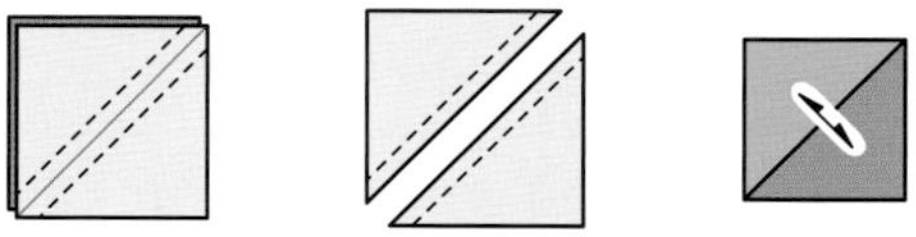

Make 4.

2. Layer two half-square-triangle units, right sides together, with the brown triangle facing the gold triangle. Draw a diagonal line perpendicular to the seam on the top unit. Sew ¼" from both sides of the line. Cut on the line to yield two hourglass units. Make four identical hourglass units. Trim each unit to 2½" square.

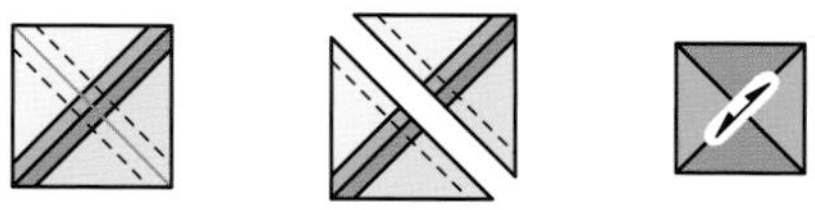

Make 4 units,
2½" × 2½".

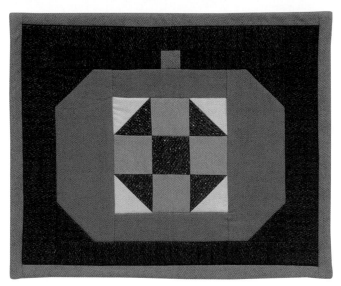

3 Lay out the hourglass units, a brown tweed 2½" square, and four cream 2½" squares. Sew the pieces into rows, and then join the rows to complete an Ohio Star block that measures 6½" square, including seam allowances.

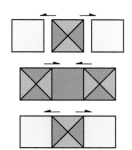

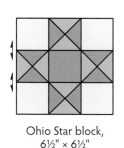

Ohio Star block,
6½" × 6½"

4 Referring to "Making the Center Blocks" on page 54, follow steps 1–6 to make one Shoofly block, one Pinwheel block, and one Variable Star block.

MAKING THE PUMPKIN BLOCKS

1 Draw a diagonal line from corner to corner on the wrong side of each espresso 2½" square. Place two marked squares on an orange 3½" × 9½" rectangle, right sides together. Sew on the lines. Cut ¼" beyond the lines; press the triangles open. Repeat to make eight side units.

Make 8 side units,
3½" × 9½".

2 Lay out the Ohio Star block, two orange 2" × 6½" rectangles, and two side units. Join the pieces to make a pumpkin unit that measures 12½" × 9½", including seam allowances.

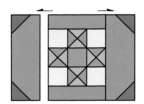

Make 1 unit,
12½" × 9½".

ASSEMBLING THE PLACE MATS

1 Lay out the pumpkin unit, two espresso 1½" × 6" rectangles, one green 1½" square, two espresso 1¾" × 12½" rectangles, and two espresso 2¼" × 13" rectangles. Join the pieces to complete a place-mat center that measures 16" × 13", including seam allowances.

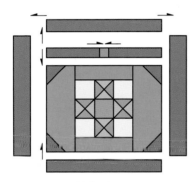

Make 1 unit,
16" × 13".

2 Sew the green 1¼" × 16" strips to the top and bottom of the place-mat center, and then add the green 1¼" × 14½" strips to the sides. The place mat should measure 17½" × 14½", including seam allowances.

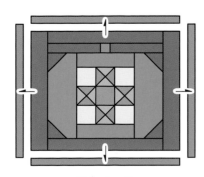

Make 1 unit,
17½" × 14½".

3 Repeat to make three more place-mat tops using the Shoofly, Pinwheel, and Variable Star blocks.

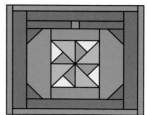

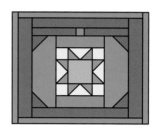

Make 1 of each,
17½" × 14½".

FINISHING THE PLACE MATS

1 To make the backing, sew two flannel 9¼" × 14½" rectangles together along their long edges, using a ½" seam allowance and leaving an opening in the center of the seam for turning. Press the seam allowances open. The backing should measure 14½" × 17½"

2 Layer and pin a pieced backing rectangle and a place-mat top, right sides together. Place the pieces on top of a batting rectangle with the place mat top against the batting.

3 Stitch around the perimeter of the place mat using a ¼" seam allowance. Trim the batting even with the edge of the place mat and backing. Trim the corners and turn the place mat right side out; press. Sew the opening closed.

4 Quilt by hand or machine. The place mats shown are machine quilted in the ditch. The center blocks are unquilted. Stitch in the ditch between the place-mat center and the green border strips for the look of binding.

Autumn Patch Quilt

~~~~~~~~ designed and pieced by BONNIE SULLIVAN ~~~~~~~~

Traditional Ohio Star blocks stitched in warm shades of pumpkin and butterscotch sparkle across this inviting flannel quilt that's sure to be a family favorite. Easy pieced setting triangles frame the design.

Finished quilt: 76⅞" × 89½"
Finished block: 9" × 9"

MATERIALS

Fabrics used in this quilt are Woolies flannels from Maywood Studio. Yardage is based on 42"-wide fabric. Fat quarters are 18" × 21".

- 4¼ yards of olive herringbone for setting squares and triangles

- 3¼ yards of espresso tweed for blocks and binding

- 1 fat quarter *each* of 6 rust prints (windowpane, plaid, herringbone, houndstooth, tiny houndstooth, and rust with black dots) for blocks

- 7⅛ yards of flannel for backing

- 85" × 97" piece of batting

CUTTING

From the olive herringbone, cut:
2 strips, 10" × 42"; crosscut into:
   6 squares, 10" × 10"; cut into quarters diagonally to
     yield 24 quarter-square triangles (2 are extra)
   2 squares, 7¼" × 7¼"; cut in half diagonally to yield
     4 half-square triangles
11 strips, 9½" × 42"; crosscut into 42 squares, 9½" × 9½"
2 strips, 6½" × 42"

From the espresso tweed:
8 strips, 4½" × 42"; crosscut into 60 squares, 4½" × 4½"
13 strips, 3½" × 42"; crosscut *11* strips into 120 squares,
   3½" × 3½". Set remaining 2 strips aside.
9 strips, 2½" × 42"

From *each* fat quarter, cut:
3 strips, 4½" × 21"; crosscut into 10 squares, 4½" × 4½"
   (60 total)
1 strip, 3½" × 21"; crosscut into 5 squares, 3½" × 3½"
   (30 total)

MAKING THE BLOCKS

Press the seam allowances as indicated by the arrows.

1   Draw a diagonal line from corner to corner on the wrong side of each rust 4½" square. Place a marked square on a rust 4½" square, right sides together. Sew ¼" from both sides of the line. Cut along the line to yield two half-square-triangle units that measure 4⅛" square.

Make 2 units,
4⅛" × 4⅛".

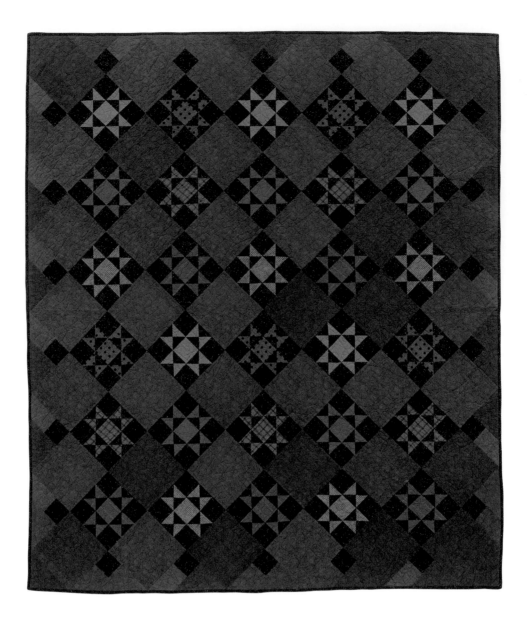

2 Layer the half-square-triangle units right sides together, with the rust triangles on top of the espresso triangles. Draw a diagonal line perpendicular to the seam on the wrong side of the top unit. Sew ¼" from both sides of the line. Cut along the line to yield two hourglass units; press. Trim the hourglass units to 3½" square.

Make 2 units,
3½" × 3½".

3 Repeat steps 1 and 2 to make a total of 120 hourglass units, 20 of each rust print.

4 Lay out one set of four matching hourglass units, one matching rust 3½" square, and four espresso 3½" squares in three rows as shown. Sew the pieces together into rows, and then sew the rows together to make a block that measures 9½" square, including seam allowances. Make 30 blocks.

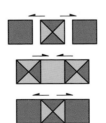

Make 30 blocks,
9½" × 9½".

MAKING THE SETTING UNITS

1 Sew one olive 6½"-wide strip and one espresso 3½"-wide strip together to make a strip set. Make two strip sets. Crosscut the strip sets into 22 segments, 3½" wide.

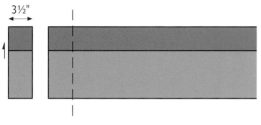

Make 2 strip sets, 9½" × 42".
Cut 11 segments, 3½" × 9½", from each.

2 Sew an olive quarter-square triangle to a segment to make a setting unit as shown. Make 22.

Make 22.

ASSEMBLING THE QUILT TOP

1 Lay out the blocks, olive 9½" squares, and setting units in diagonal rows as shown in the quilt assembly diagram below.

2 Join the pieces into diagonal rows. Join the rows. Sew an olive half-square triangle to each corner.

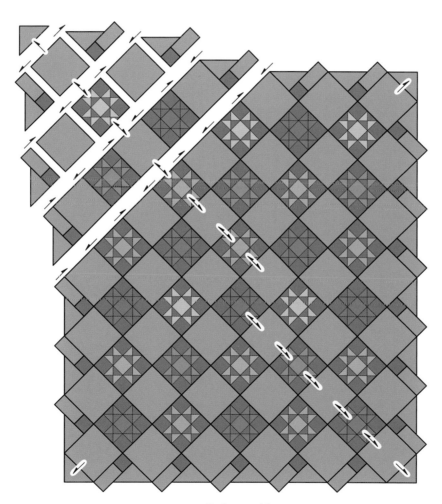

Quilt assembly

3 Trim the sides of the quilt top, leaving a ¼" seam allowance beyond the points of the olive squares as shown.

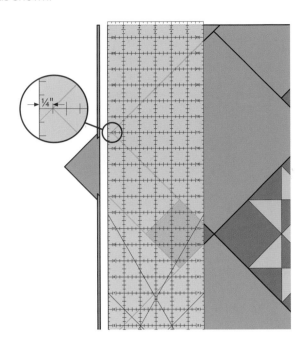

Stay Stitch Those Edges

Sew around the perimeter of the quilt top, within the seam allowance, to prevent the seams from coming unsewn while quilting.

FINISHING THE QUILT

1 Cut the backing fabric into three 85" lengths. Sew the pieces together side by side.

2 Layer and baste the backing, batting, and quilt top. Quilt by hand or machine. The quilt shown is machine quilted with an allover pattern of free-motion stars and loops.

3 Use the espresso 2½"-wide strips to make a double-fold binding, and then attach the binding to the quilt.

Pumpkin Head Whatnots

designed and made by BONNIE SULLIVAN

Quilters who like to work with wool tend to love "whatnots" or
"make-dos," like these handsome guys. You can set them on a table to add to
your fall decor or perch each one on a candlestick pedestal atop a ruffled collar.

Off-white pumpkin: 7½" diameter × 9" tall

Orange pumpkin: 6" diameter × 12" tall

MATERIALS

Materials are for 1 pumpkin.

- 16" × 16" square of orange plaid *OR* off-white wool for pumpkin head

- 7½" × 7½" square of olive wool for hat *OR* 4" × 8" piece of gold wool for stem

- 2½" × 30" strip of purple wool for collar *OR* 6" × 42" strip of orange flannel or cotton fabric for collar

- 3" × 3" square of purple wool for polka dots on hat (optional)

- Scraps of wool in black, red, orange, and white for mouth, nose, and eyes

- Thread in black, red, white, and color to match stem or hat

- Wool floss in black

- 2 black buttons, ½" diameter

- Fiberfill for stuffing

- Wooden candlestick and black craft paint (optional)

- Glue gun, optional

- 8" length of green chenille yarn for hat

- Freezer paper

CUTTING

Make freezer-paper templates using the patterns on pattern sheet 4.

From the orange plaid wool *OR* off-white wool, cut:
6 pumpkin A pieces *OR* 6 pumpkin B pieces

From the olive wool, cut:,
1 hat (optional)

From the gold wool, cut:
2 stem pieces (optional)

PREPARING THE APPLIQUÉS

Trace the appliqué shapes using the patterns on pattern sheet 4 onto freezer paper and cut out on the marked lines. Refer to the patterns for which fabrics to use.

SEWING THE PUMPKIN HEAD

1 Sew three matching head sections together to make half of the head. Start and stop sewing at the dot on the pattern and backstitch at each end. Make the other half in the same manner. Join the halves, matching all of the seams at the top and leaving an opening in the bottom for turning.

Leave open.

2 Turn the head right side out and stuff lightly. Don't sew the opening closed.

3 Choose the middle section of one side of the head for the face pieces. Pin the pieces in place and then whipstitch the eyes, nose, and mouth to that side using thread in matching colors. Hide the knots by pulling them through to the inside, and refer to the photo for placement as necessary.

4 Use black wool floss to outline stitch around the eyes and the nose. Sew a ½" black button to the center of each eye.

5 Finish stuffing the head to the desired firmness and sew the bottom opening closed.

6 If you're making the stem, sew the stem pieces right sides together. Trim the seam allowances, turn right side out, and stuff. Turn under the edge and whipstitch the stem in place on top of the head.

7 If you're making the hat, sew the polka dots to the surface of the olive wool hat piece in a random manner. Sew the hat right sides together along the straight edges to form a cone. Turn right side out and stuff. Sew the hat to the top of the head. Sew a strand of chenille yarn along the seam where the hat meets the head.

8 If you're making the wool collar, run a gathering stitch along one edge of the purple wool strip and whipstitch the ends together. Pull the thread until the gathered edge forms a 2" diameter circle in the center. Hot glue or stitch the collar to the bottom of the pumpkin, centering the open circle at the bottom of the pumpkin head.

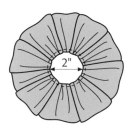

9 If you're making the flannel collar, sew the strip right sides together along its short edges to form a ring. Fold the ring in half lengthwise, *wrong* sides together so that the flannel print is on the outside. Run a basting stitch along the unfinished edges and pull the thread ends until the gathered edge forms a 2" diameter circle in the center. Attach the collar as described in step 8 for the wool collar.

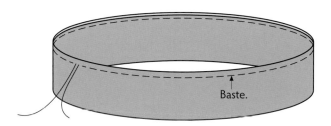

Baste.

10 If desired, use a glue gun to adhere the bottom of the pumpkin head to a wooden candlestick.

Painting Wooden Candlesticks

Lightly sand the candlesticks to smooth any rough spots, then wipe off the sanding dust. Paint the wood with a thin coat of paint and let dry. Paint raises the wood grain, so you might need to lightly sand again. Give the candlesticks a second coat and let the paint dry.

Woolie Nine-Patch Quilt

 designed and pieced by BONNIE SULLIVAN

Cool, crisp fall days and even chillier nights call for a comforting flannel throw that's perfect to wrap up in. Classic Double Nine Patch blocks are always in season, and especially so when set on point.

Finished quilt: 69¼" × 85⅛"
Finished block: 11¼" × 11¼"

MATERIALS

Fabrics used in this quilt are Woolies flannels from Maywood Studio. Yardage is based on 44"-wide fabric. Fat quarters are 18" × 22". Do not prewash the flannel fabrics as they will shrink and you won't have sufficient yardage.

- ⅞ yard of orange houndstooth for blocks
- 2½ yards of espresso tweed for blocks and outer border
- 1½ yards of green basketweave for blocks, inner border, and binding
- 1 fat quarter *each* of 4 prints (blue, light brown, purple, and red) for blocks
- 1⅞ yards of espresso houndstooth for alternate blocks and setting triangles
- 5¼ yards of flannel for backing
- 77" × 93" piece of batting

CUTTING

From the orange houndstooth, cut:
6 strips, 4¼" × 44"; crosscut into 48 squares, 4¼" × 4¼"

From the espresso tweed, cut:
8 strips, 8" × 44"
10 strips, 1¾" × 44"; cut each strip in half to make 2 strips. 1¾" × 22" (20 total)

From the green basketweave, cut:
6 strips, 3½" × 44"
9 strips, 2½" × 44"
3 strips, 1¾" × 44"; cut each strip in half to make 2 strips, 1¾" × 22" (6 total, 1 is extra)

From *each* fat quarter, cut:
5 strips, 1¾" × 22" (20 total)

From the espresso houndstooth, cut:
2 strips, 17¼" × 44"; crosscut into:
  3 squares, 17¼" × 17¼"; cut into quarters diagonally to make 12 side setting triangles (2 are extra)
  2 squares, 8⅞" × 8⅞"; cut in half diagonally to make 4 corner setting triangles
2 strips, 11¾" × 44"; crosscut into 6 squares, 11¾" × 11¾"

MAKING THE BLOCKS

Press the seam allowances open or as indicated by the arrows.

1 Sew two green 22"-long strips and one espresso 22"-long strip together to make strip set A as shown. Make two strip sets. Cut a total of 24 A segments, 1¾" wide.

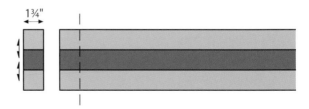

Strip set A. Make 2 strip sets, 4¼" × 22".
Cut 24 segments, 1¾" × 4¼".

2 Sew two espresso 22"-long strips and one green 22"-long strip together to make strip set B as shown. Cut a total of 12 B segments, 1¾" wide.

Strip set B. Make 1 strip set, 4¼" × 22".
Cut 12 segments, 1¾" × 4¼".

3 Lay out two A segments and one B segment. Join the segments to make a green nine-patch unit that measures 4¼" square, including seam allowances. Make 12 matching nine-patch units.

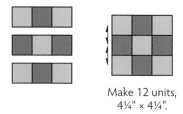

Make 12 units,
4¼" × 4¼".

4 Repeat steps 1–3 to make 12 nine-patch units each of blue, purple, light brown, and red.

5 Lay out five nine-patch units (one of each color) and four orange 4¼" squares in three rows. Join the pieces into rows; join the rows to complete a Double Nine Patch block that measures 11¾" square, including seam allowances. Make 12 blocks.

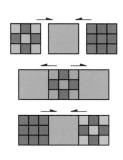
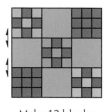

Make 12 blocks,
11¾" × 11¾".

ASSEMBLING THE QUILT TOP

1 Lay out the blocks, the espresso 11¾" squares, the setting triangles, and the corner triangles.

2 Join the pieces into diagonal rows and join the rows.

3 Join the green 3½"-wide strips end to end. Measure the length of the quilt through the center. From the pieced strip, cut two borders to this length. Sew the borders to the sides of the quilt center; press.

4 Measure the width of the quilt through the center, including the borders just added. From the pieced strip, cut two borders to this length. Sew the borders to the top and bottom of the quilt top; press.

5 Repeat steps 3 and 4 to add the espresso 8"-wide outer border to the quilt.

FINISHING THE QUILT

1 Cut the backing fabric in half to make two 94" lengths. Sew the pieces together side by side.

2 Layer and baste the backing, batting, and quilt top. Quilt by hand or machine. The quilt shown is machine quilted with leaves in the borders, nested stars and nine-patch grids in the dark squares and triangles, and swirls in the Nine Patch blocks.

3 Use the green 2½"-wide strips to make a double-fold binding. Attach the binding to the quilt.

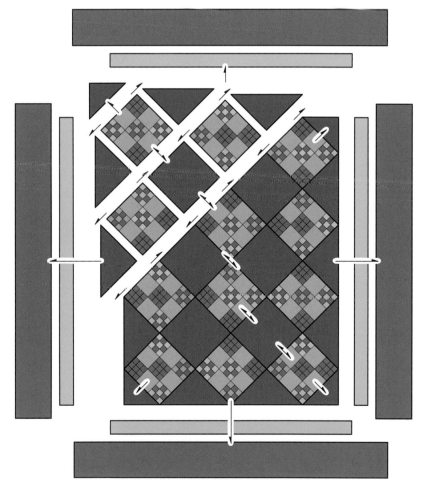

Quilt assembly

Autumn's Bounty Pillow

designed and made by BONNIE SULLIVAN

Capture the luscious colors of harvest season in a
rich-looking pillow. All that nature has to offer meets a
whimsical twist with the addition of two impish squirrels.

Finished size: 16" × 16"

MATERIALS

- 17" × 17" square of black wool for pillow top
- 17" × 17" square of black wool or flannel for pillow back
- 8" × 10" rectangle of gray tweed wool for squirrels
- 6" × 11" rectangle of gray-and-white check wool for fruit bowl
- 5" × 6" rectangle of orange wool for pumpkin
- 4" × 6½" rectangle of light yellow wool for squash
- 5" × 8" rectangle of green plaid wool for oak leaves
- 2½" × 5" rectangle of dark green solid wool for apple leaf, grape leaf, and pumpkin stem
- 3" × 3" square of light brown solid wool for acorns
- 3" × 3" square of brown tweed wool for acorn caps
- 1" × 6" rectangle of dark brown solid wool for oak stems
- 3½" × 3½" square of pear green wool for pear
- 3" × 3" square of red wool for apple
- 3½" × 4" rectangle of purple wool for grapes
- 1½" × 1½" square of rusty red wool for berries
- Thread in colors to match wools
- Pearl cotton in black and brown
- 2 yards of orange fringe trim for pillow edges
- Paper-backed fusible web
- 16" square pillow form or stuffing of your choice

PREPARING THE APPLIQUÉS

Referring to "Appliqué with Fusible Web" on page 78,
prepare the appliqué shapes using the patterns on
pattern sheet 4. Refer to the patterns for which fabrics
to use. For the oak stems, cut one piece, ¼" × 5¾", and
one piece, ¼" × 2¾", from the dark brown solid wool; do
not fuse these pieces.

STITCHING THE APPLIQUÉS

See page 79 for embroidery stitch instructions. Fuse the pieces in place according to the manufacturer's instructions.

1 Referring to the photo on page 76, arrange the appliqué pieces on the black wool square, taking care to tuck some pieces over or under others as designated. Fuse and whipstitch in place using threads that match the appliqué pieces.

2 Use brown pearl cotton to outline stitch three rows right next to one another to create the stems of the apple and pear. Stitch two rows of side-by-side outline stitches to make the stems on the acorns.

3 Use black pearl cotton to stitch a French knot eye on each squirrel.

FINISHING THE PILLOW

1 Align the straight edge of the fringe trim with the outside edge of the pillow top and sew it in place all the way around the perimeter using a ⅜" seam allowance. Overlap the ends and trim off the excess.

2 Layer the pillow front and back pieces, right sides together. Using a ½" seam allowance, sew around the pillow pieces. Leave an opening along the bottom edge for turning and stuffing.

3 Clip the corners, turn right side out, and insert the 16" pillow form (or fiberfill). Whipstitch the opening closed.

A Few Basics about Wool Appliqué

Wool appliqué is easy and so much fun. Over the years, I've tried many different ways of preparing the pieces for appliqué and many different stitches, and I've settled on the following techniques.

APPLIQUÉ WITH FUSIBLE WEB

1 Patterns are reversed for use with fusible web. Trace the patterns onto the paper side of lightweight fusible web, and cut out the shapes roughly ⅛" to ¼" outside the traced lines.

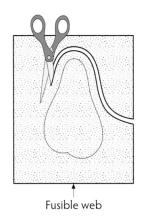

Fusible web

2 Place the paper shapes on the wrong side of the designated fabric and fuse in place following the manufacturer's instructions. Cut out the pieces on the lines.

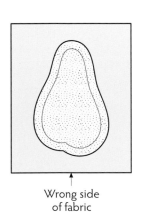
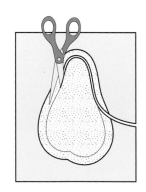

Wrong side of fabric

3 Peel the paper off the shapes and arrange them on the appropriate fabrics; press to fuse the shapes to the fabric. When using fusible web with wool, you may have to give it a little more time and pressure to make sure the heat goes through the thick wool, especially when there are multiple layers. Because the wool is thick, pressing from the back after you've pressed the front will help the glue to adhere.

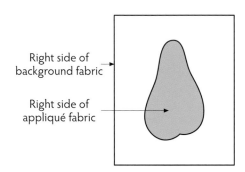

Right side of background fabric

Right side of appliqué fabric

4 Stitch the shapes to the fabric as described in the project instructions.

WHIPSTITCHING

Whipstitches are used to hold the pieces in place. Some appliqué pieces are whipstitched with coordinating thread only, and others are embellished with another thread, such as pearl cotton or wool floss.

Try to make the stitches the same length as the distance between them, as shown below.

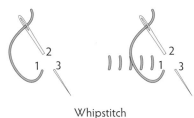

Whipstitch

OTHER STITCHES USED

For the blanket stitch, try to keep the stitches on the front
of your piece perpendicular to the edge, as shown below.

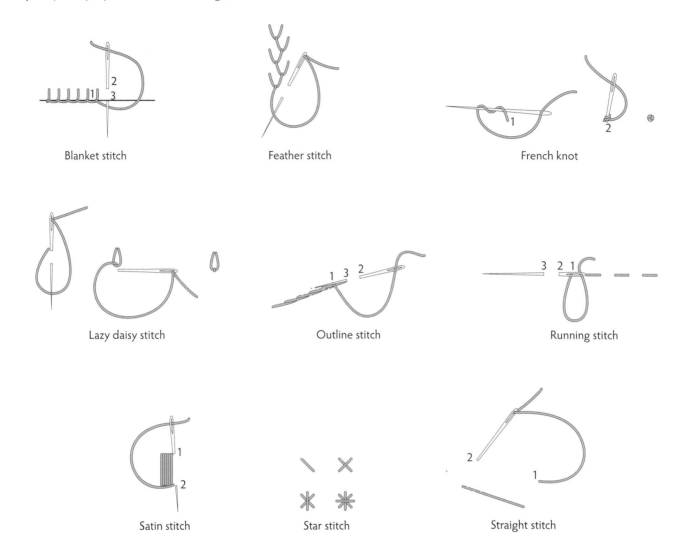

Blanket stitch

Feather stitch

French knot

Lazy daisy stitch

Outline stitch

Running stitch

Satin stitch

Star stitch

Straight stitch

Meet the Author

For as long as I can remember, I've always loved textiles—I still have remnants of my childhood blanket. My neighbor taught me how to embroider when I was seven. My mother taught 4-H sewing, and I spent many childhood hours making troll and Barbie doll clothes. I remember being fascinated by the quilts my grandmother and mother pieced and hand quilted. There is just something comforting about working with fabrics and wools, and the textures and colors have captivated me from a very young age. I never thought I'd be designing and creating for a living, but I'm thankful every day for the opportunity.

I was introduced to working with wool in 2000 and was immediately hooked. After designing several penny-rug patterns, I thought I would try my luck at the International Quilt Market and attended my first show as a vendor in May of 2002. My business quickly grew and in 2003, I began designing fabric for Maywood Studio. Because I love working with wool, I designed a line of flannels called Woolies to look like wool. The Woolies line has gone through many transformations over the years, adding new colors and textures. I love combining the Woolies flannels with wool, and many of the projects in this book are made with a combination of the two. Please visit my website at AllThroughtheNight.net.

7